For the Boy with the Eyes of the Virgin

ALSO BY JOHN BARTON

POETRY

A Poor Photographer
Hidden Structure
West of Darkness: Emily Carr, a Self-Portrait
Great Men
Notes Toward a Family Tree
Designs from the Interior
Sweet Ellipsis
Hypothesis
Hymn

POETRY CHAPBOOKS

Destinations, Leaving the Map
Oxygen
Shroud
Runoff
Asymmetries (In the House of the Present and *The Strata)*
Balletomane: The Program Notes of Lincoln Kirsten

EDITOR

Silences
belles lettres / beautiful letters
We All Begin in a Little Magazine: Arc and the Promise of Canada's Poets, 1978–1998
Seminal: The Anthology of Canada's Gay Male Poets

IN TRANSLATION

À l'ouest de l'ombre: Emily Carr, un autoportrait

For the Boy with the Eyes of the Virgin

Selected Poems

John Barton

Nightwood Editions
2012

Nightwood Editions
P.O. Box 1779
Gibsons, BC VON 1VO
Canada
www.nightwoodeditions.com

TYPOGRAPHY & DESIGN: Carleton Wilson
COVER IMAGE: Miles Lowry, *Within*
(cast and painted cotton fibre), 2009.
www.mileslowry.ca

Nightwood Editions acknowledges financial support from the Government of Canada through the Canada Book Fund and the Canada Council for the Arts, and from the Province of British Columbia through the British Columbia Arts Council and the Book Publisher's Tax Credit.

This book has been produced on 100% post-consumer recycled, ancient-forest-free paper, processed chlorine-free and printed with vegetable-based dyes.

Printed and bound in Canada.

LIBRARY AND ARCHIVES CANADA CATALOGUING IN PUBLICATION

Barton, John, 1957–
For the boy with the eyes of the virgin : selected poems / John Barton.

ISBN 978-0-88971-270-6

I. Title.

PS8553.A78F67 2012 C811'.54 C2012-903573-4

"What happens in the heart simply happens."

—Ted Hughes

CONTENTS

"I NO LONGER FEAR TO BE A MAN" OR, THE JOHN BARTON GUIDE TO BETTER LIVING

R. M. Vaughan

I no longer fear to be a man
and we are lovers whether our lovers
are women or men.

—from "Naked Hearts"

I CANNOT WRITE ABOUT the poetry of John Barton. I can easily, however, write about the poetries of John Barton. Indeed, I luxuriate in Bartonian pluralities.

First, a personal note. John Barton and I have been friends for years. He's a naturally thoughtful, considerate sort, but hardly a saint—the man can bitch and dish with the best of us. Like me, he's gay, abundantly gay, in all the miraculous and sparkly and arch and flamboyant and angry and queer and off-kilter and hilarious and too-creative-for-his-own-good senses of the adjective. He's a bit of a perv, too—but you'll figure that out soon enough, dear reader.

Oddly, I cannot remember where or how John and I first met. That is not a reflection on John's ability to make social, but rather my own ability to erase and recreate history, memory, and all their micro-dramas, to suit my own needs. So, I will say that John and I met in Paris, at a perfume store, wherein we advised and consulted on the merits of ambergris over musk, lilac over pine. You call me absent-minded, I call myself creative.

But I wonder if one of the reasons I can't remember how John and I met is because, as noted above, there are many John Bartons? (Poetically speaking, of course. I'm not a shrink.)

John's poetry, as evidenced in the three decades of work sampled here—yes, three decades of writing poetry...unpack that bravery, that sheer raging audacity, at your own leisure—offers the reader everything from skinny, sexy erotic hymns to form-bending diary prose poems to *J'accuse!* rants in ghazals to polyphonic post-Pop queer theory dialogues. And that ain't the half of it.

The poetry collected in this survey is but a small dollop of John's voluminous output. John writes poetry the way some people write emails—daily, and by the handful. Genius is volume, I always say. But it's the material that really matters, not the heft—and John's place in Canada's poetics geography, and history, is unquestionable, because there is no such thing as a cowardly John Barton poem.

A John Barton poem was "out" long before it was safe, out in an era when publishers would print any old sweet cream and teatime-recipe poem or muddy-boot cowboy ode (and not my kind of cowboy) before they'd letterset a simple love song between two fellows.

Indeed, a John Barton poem openly questioned essentialist readings of poetry, the idea that poems could be gendered—arguably, his poems did more than question gender essentialism, they tossed the idea out the window, let flossy silk curtains and manly wooden blinds both sail to the ground where they were run over and mud-pie-flattened by trucks, trucks driven by tough dykes.

A John Barton poem fearlessly told the world that, yes, oh yes, some of us menfolk like to make love to other men, and we are very good at it, and the poems we make to mark this simple reality can also express related ideas of gender, identity, masculinity (and its decodings), and all the anxieties created by such expressions, via an endless, and enviable, spectrum of presentation strategies, arrangements of words, love(s) put to the page.

A John Barton poem is therefore, by its sheer complexity if not the honest stories it tells, a gay poem, a queerness writ epic, or in sing-song, or compact diorama-like apostrophe, or in ladders of line, chain mail.

A John Barton poem is also, of course, not a gay poem—because any poet as devoted to unveiling the unreliability of form and content as measures, ways of label-sticking, would never agree to be read one way, nor be capable of making a poem that could ever be read only one way.

A John Barton poem is, then, an interventionist act, a drag (in all gender directions) performance staged in Canadian poetry's musty, briny Legion Hall, a poem just asking for trouble. John was "queer" before the word became the *Open Sesame!* to tenure, and its subsidiary safeties.

•

"I no longer fear to be a man"....

When I first read that line, I thought: yes, that is it, that's the defining moment in one's life (however you self-define: man, woman, all or neither), the second when one decides that a life of fear is a finished-before-it-starts life, not to mention a crashing bore.

Self-definition, by definition, is a rejection of fear, an assertion of the undeniable, a gauntlet drop. Some of us gently arrange the gauntlet, that jewelled glove that signals the brawl between you and the whole goddamned world, on the mat floor, some of us hurl it at the crowd, and some of us tie the fingers into exquisite knots, make ascots of the fourchettes. You can guess which gang John belongs to (in any given moment).

Risking reductionism, I posit that John's poems all share, in part or whole, this defining action, and/or wish to impart said action to others. In every line, we read John's self-affirmation as a gift, an act of outreach, if you will (an unfortunate word, outreach, so co-opted by do-gooders): a poem-cum-communiqué that alerts the reader to the potential within (s)himself to fully become, to unfold, blossom. And, yes, to accept the consequences of living a life engorged, inattentive to boundaries (but hardly finesse).

Self-affirmation is not without its risks, and John meets them with clean, hammer-brutal honesty. This is not poetry for people who believe in better futures, but rather for people already on the cusp of the future tense. People who understand that to live so, life (and poetry) demand we know grief as well as joy, rage and love, remorse and its opposite, orgasm.

I no longer fear to be a man, but I once did.

Poetry—writing it, reading it, speaking it out loud—manned me up. Sure, by "manned me up" I also and of course mean, to name but a few guises, dressed me up, in the most luscious ball gowns, rattiest wigs and, now and then, a spot of not convincing but earnest rawhide ... but we've already covered that whole Gender 101 issue.

Writing poetry makes one brave, stupid, prone to romantic misadventure, and, best of all, alert.

John Barton is the most alert poet I know. He misses nothing, his poetry even less. Read a John Barton poem and find a world encapsulated, held close, closer than a lover, but never asphyxiated. John's poems breathe, pulse, occasionally bark, and always, always bite. They do this because they no longer fear to be; a man or whatever's going around.

Lifeblood is pumped into a poem (or, in the book you now hold in your hands, a poetic practice) at exactly the moment fear sighs out of the veins, when fear is transplanted (pardon the operating-room pun) with agency. Agency, the poet's best friend.

Agency works outwardly too. I don't care if you're a heterosexual garbage-scow worker with nine children and a dog named Butch, you get John Barton.

You understand that to be who you want to be, you have to *say* who you want to be, to yourself, or out loud, or to the swirling gulls even—or it will never happen, and you'll be someone else.

John Barton's poetry makes the old adage about the specific invoking the universal look like a moth-eaten standard framed in tarnished silver. John's poetry does not invoke the universal, it follows from a core belief that attaining universality is to be expected, is part and parcel of the act of writing—anybody can do that.

But such spectacular specifics? That's the magic part.

A great poet knows the angels (and the fairies, all the sparkling species) are in—and sprout from, question, and certainly honour—the details.

For the Boy with the Eyes of the Virgin

1981: Two Poems from *A Poor Photographer*

THE PREGNANT MAN

I've let you in,
filled empty marble halls,
arching silences that have lasted generations.
My doctors will be shocked.
Hitler will be shocked.
They never knew I would give birth
to a new age.

You who festered into an unaborted spore,
ate like a maggot into my sarcophagus,
you grew, became an electric storm,
a nuclear threat.

The first month, morning sickness.
I became an occupied country.
I never sensed the missiles cross the border.

The second month I knew for sure.
You became amorphous,
swallowed my genitalia, my heart, my belly.

The third month doctors fed me pills,
Morse code to negotiate my surrender.
I jammed all frequencies,
refused to get the message.

The fourth month you broke radio silence.
Pleased with my progress,
they decoded your movements,
made plans to revive me.

My nerves became slow fuses,
exploding into recurring dreams of afterbirths
drooling over coat hangers,
like last year's Sunday best.

The fifth month you were Stalin,
holidaying in Crimea, sending me memos in Siberia.
You offered asylum; I accused you of treason.

By the sixth month you had deposed me,
set up interim government.
I felt as Napoleon did
plotting revolution in the dark on Elba.

During the seventh month I hid in the catacombs;
you lurked still deeper.
When you threatened to lash me to a stake,
I knew then my plans would go up in an arc of flame.

The eighth month, heavy with you, I relented.
You paraded me to the gallows.
I was left in wonderland,
hanging
in suspense.

Nine months after the first jolt,
you mushroomed forth, an icon, a holocaust.
The world melted through my eyes,
entered into my thoughts.
You left me comatose.
It was all new, all over.

Observers tell me I'm a new man.
I surface once or twice, almost gone,
The third time, it's your hand that grabs me.

An act of allegiance you say; I still fear reprisals.
Oppressed I'm a dissident, an isolationist.
You send out search parties; I leave false trails.
Your propaganda, your six o'clock news,
proposes ceasefire, even mediation.
You plead recognition; I veto all peace talks.
Some day you'll coerce me into submission, I'll start
to believe all that shit about being lovers,
being friends.

A POOR PHOTOGRAPHER IMPROVES HIS VISION

I

in my dark room last night
I developed a
picture of you last summer
all winter I kept another
wedged under the frame of
my mirror
our eyes met at eye
level

only when I tinted your face
white
when I bleached out all
your features
did the negative come into
perspective
on the print
your face printed
black
your eyes cast
a black light

II

nights I spend asleep
I spend

walking through forests still clothed
in their snows, exposed

to their cold light, shadows
uncoil

vines from your eyes, finger
the soft

belly of my thoughts.
I prefer

the leaves your touch shook free
of, the islands

risen between us, the excuses
your lips gave

mine.
I prefer the illusion of dawn

the wind ravels from the copper light
of copper beech trees

to sunlight itself. I prefer the
shimmering

guilt of my leaving
to the harsh electric light

waking
limply above my bed, its light sifting

over me like snow.
I prefer the shadow of your breath

to this dazzling linen
that forces my fixed eyes to

blink, change their focus.

III

abandon is an action I leave
to others
        all week I have answered no
        telephone
        calls   I have thrown out all
        my mail
                    all photographs that trace the contours
                    of your dark
                    love
                          I have pasted against the negative
                    side of my mirror
                          my eyes stare into their echoes
                          into their own
                          empty solars

I prefer the perfected
symmetry of bare walls

the painted-in corners of your
absence

IV

without your eyes merging with my own dark

without your fingers smoothing my lips into focus

without your breath exposing the topography of my skin

I have time for the clear blue of my thoughts

I have time for the clear distances between us

I have time for the glassy-eyed texture of my anger

1984: *Hidden Structure*

HIDDEN STRUCTURE

After he left I put on shorts and walked along the beach
and looked at the palms curving away from the ocean.
My old adolescent feeling that it was odd to be a man
rather than a woman, to live here rather than there,
now rather than then, struck me again. I wanted to
hurtle through space and time.

—Edmund White

Though my heart aches, this
immensity of quiet, of trees
simply reaching into sky
is of such gravity it lures me,

is sufficient to defeat me, defeat
my need to be clear. The flowers
unfold, mirror
the slanted path of the sun.

I arrive at the sea. It repeats me,
repeats me. Yes,
the sun draws itself out, the wave
crests shaving it down,

first to a spark, then to an ash.
The quiet so inviolable
my voice invokes
nothing but terror. And yet I return,

and return to my rooms.
Nothing's begun.
Friends, though ceaselessly
the same, change,

repeat themselves.
                    Do I love, then?
Do I love?
The sea remains inextricable

like a god.
Its memory is the pause
in my heart.
Thy will be done.

My rooms unravel their quiet
like ripples from a stone thrown
inside me. Their shadows as they spread
swallow the garden I thought

I would raise myself in. And the sun,
the bloody sun, as it rises
is nothing but darkness. It draws
the sea out of itself,

leaves a ridge of salt along the inside
of my windows.
I wake.
The telephone rings.

All is the same.

•

I know a woman who has crawled inside
the alarming shell of herself,
her voice a faint shock of sea over the phone.
What she never says

tightens like lightning voluptuous
in its fist of cloud. What she says
is gentle as rain against the window pane,
calla lilies refusing to bend

to the pent-up ground.
She is proud. Her walks never end
by the sea.
I let her hang up,

see her curled on the bed
reading, the folds of her dress
arranged like petals, just so,
on her knees. She looks up,

pretends not to breathe, pretends
the story she is reading is more
than print on the page. Her room
is a cell within a cell

within the seed of a flower. Its growth
is a wave almost willing
to break. She is nearly ready to say,
I want this, I want this,

meaning she does, meaning she doesn't.

•

And then there is another
from the interior;
his mountains and lakes hold him
no longer in the cradle of his

first thoughts. The forests
that helped shape him he slowly
helped fell. He left them.
Their needles fall

from his heart. Even the company of men
in the work camps and the women
spun into their yarns
by the fire (each one a wild card they cut

out of their lives) slip from him
like water as a swimmer
stumbles on shore and into the dark.
He is not used to sea fog.

He seldom goes home,
but each night crosses the threshold
of his thoughts and lives
by himself. He walks by the sea.

He never looks me straight
in the eye, tells me
of each woman he's loved and how
each one lost the path to his heart.

He never looks me straight
in the eye. His darkly haired hands
gripping his beer. His chest
tenses, relaxes under his pale blue shirt.

What his gaze fixes on
is never mirrored in his eyes.
I look down at my hands,
then look straight ahead.

He is smiling.

•

And then there's me who lives without
my mother. She lives without
my father. Whatever she dreamed
of his love was extinguished

like the sun by the ocean's slow tug.
She stretches to fill
their forty-year bed, her reading lamp
dim. What she cannot let go of

she polishes like stones in her
hands, each one featureless—
she can't even remember their names.
She reads to lose whole

strands of herself,
but he is still
the rack of desire speeding her blood
and makes her want

to cry out, cry for her mother.
I want to tell her,
Mother, we all sleep by ourselves,
but I can't. We have destroyed in living

alone the meaning of love.
I want to tell you
we all share the brevity
of another's flesh when we can

and for a moment fire the cracked
privacy of our hearts.
I want to tell you
the stories you spoon-fed me

are wrong. I am no shining knight.
My tongue hangs from my mouth,
my cock is hard,
and my bedroom is grey.

I want to tell you I love you,
but can't. We are all
children unable to cry.
Though my heart aches, it is

a stone rough with too little use.
Mother, tell me your story
of pain, of the one man you found
and the other you lost.

Mother, I am young.
We are drifting apart.
Forgive me this sin.
Something is missing.

•

Something is missing.
We are all approximate beings
made proximate by love.
The sun lures us together—

it lures us apart. Whether we will it,
or defy it, the sun
lures us in or
out of the anguish of dark.

Yet there are moments of clarity
so sheer I am sure I can
love without fear. The will bursts open
like the shutters and lets in

the sun and the sea and the cliffs.
I am sure
all I know is
hidden on purpose, kept

like a seed,
                or a thorn,
beneath the perfect mirror of the sea
at the back of my mind.

•

What is missing is this:
I also love men
with marble-
hard flesh that melts like salt

on the tongue. *I love men…*
And women…
At least I know that I've tried.
But in the grip of my ribs

all I desire to admit to
I fear.
        Don't listen.
Listen instead

to the sea, how it erodes me.
It erodes me.
For a moment I'm free.
But in the lock

of each wave as it links
with the shore
I can just hear the loss caught
in my voice.

Should I only love women?
I am forever unsure.
Their softness warms like a beach,
lures me with the promise

of flood at high tide.
Under their fingers I become
unquestionably one, at peace
as sand falls into the creases,

the cold flesh of my questions.
But men,
they are the surge and break of
luxuriant storm. I am

drawn into the vortex
whether I will it or not.
What is this power?
We sink into each other,

emerge into the calm
glittering stretch of our arms.
Do I really want this?
What structures my flesh?

Tell me before mind
and heart finish
their division and are two
autonomous cells forever

at war. Tell me.
I don't want to be their
flotsam carried from shore
by the tug of the moon.

Tell me the stories of Adam
and Eve we were given
as children are wrong.
They may have loved in the garden,

but the gates never closed.
And their fall, their fall
was no fall at all,
and the apple was sweet.

The vengeance of man, not God,
leaves the true
story forever untold. Man made it
a riddle, a pebble

worried by the touch of countless
generations of hands.
All forms of love are forced,
smoothed into this one

inescapable stone.
By its weight we are all judged.
It coarsens my hands.
Can I love both women and men?

Tell me before the stone
falls through
my fingers unanswered
into the dark grasp

of the future. I want it
to settle here, not slip
into the palms of children.
Tell me why are we born

wanting the blessing
of our mothers and fathers
when the stories they told us
are lies. Forgive them,

and write our names into
the book of the dead.
Then burn it. New life
is brought by the tide.

Listen carefully.
Tell me
what I am trying to say.
In this age men and women

go by other names.

•

Father, tell me what I am
trying to say.
The dark of our house
has followed me here.

Its quiet has settled in the four
corners of this box
of questions I have found myself in.
They demand that you and I talk.

Father, there isn't much time.
Tell me why
as a child I often wished
I was born in female

flesh, why I found life
too stony a burden
for my boy's shoulders to carry.
Did I think women strong

because they are not afraid to be
weak?
            Tell me now.
Confusion weighs like the stone

in my groin.
The child in me with tears
in his eyes tells me
he was right all along,

but the truth I am after
is a nameless
flower whose petals, once shed,
reveal a pod of seeds,

each seed being smaller,
less vital than the memory
of the bloom.
I know that in every pod

there are a thousand potential
truths, but not all
can send roots searching the depths
of the soil. Tell me

I am right before
the child in me
dies, for he is sick from too
little light. I am afraid

to open the curtains though,
afraid of what I might see.
I am afraid of meeting my friends,
afraid of the questions

the flesh raises. Father,
my whole life
you have been too long silent.
At four I remember

you sitting broad-shouldered
at a window, alone in the last
of August's dark evening light.
My mother, your wife,

had gone out for a walk
nursing her grief.
Father, I remember how you gritted
your teeth and saw

how you refused to look
into what I took for
your hate etching wrinkles into
your reflected face. I saw

only how your eyes avoided hers
when she came in.
I didn't care where your gaze rested.
I hit you instead

to see if you ever felt pain.
When you didn't flinch
I started
to cry, would have hit you

again and again, but she caught
my wrist. My fist
went numb in her grasp.
I think now you must have watched

the crabapples she pruned
that day
fade beyond reach into the pool
of the night. I hated you

then and grew up hating
the destiny I thought my sex
prisoned me in.
Tell me now of the pain

you felt in the silence
of our house the moment
you heard a key turn in the lock,
my mother bringing her grief in,

hugging me and refusing to talk.
Father, tell me
why you never
cracked open our silences.

These days I live alone
and find I have little to say.
I am strangled with pain.
Tell me you understand.

For the first time I am
listening
to the sea in my blood.
Though my heart aches

I am teaching myself to love
when I can.
                    Father
put your head to my heart.

Though you have left my mother
alone for another
like me I believe you are learning
to break free of the shell

of yourself. For the first time
in days I find myself
sitting on driftwood at the top
of the beach. As the sun

stretches its arms above
the sky I am beginning
to throw the last stones to the sea.
Father I have no room for hate.

•

Mother, Father, bless me.
This is my story.
                              I name it
grief. After letting go

of its stones, they sank
unnoticed into the sand
floor of my heart.
Now, one after the other,

they emerge soundlessly
like ghosts
from the depths of this page.
Under a single touch

of this pen their shadows
spread, widen in rings,
soften
the ragged shore.

The stinging salt
of each wave clips at
my heels. I want
to run like a child

back into the close net
of your arms.
                    But I can't.
The facts of our lives

make me keep vigil
by the edge of the sea.
Despite the lies I have tried
to make of myself

I am your child,
no longer just a fragment of your
growing apart, but
of my growing alone.

I have never felt
with the whole of myself.
No one knows who I am.
Long after your love

for each other had ebbed,
leaving the sand
between you to dry in the sun,
to be picked over by crows

and carried off by the wind
you told me
men only love women,
women only love men.

I never once listened
to the shell of my heart
tell me
the love I carry with me

is a seed
made to bear fruit.
I tilt it to my ear
(hearing the echo of spin-

drift sifting across
the reflected face of the moon),
the love you couldn't
imagine taking root

in the garden where I began
tells me
we are all first human beings
then women and men.

It says there is no one to fault,
that I must steady my heart,
simply thrust myself on,
each step farther

from whom I once was
leaving a mark in the sand.
What lies ahead on the beach
is hidden in darkness,

but I know the path through it
is safe.
So be not afraid.
The facts of our lives

simply form
the whole of our forever growing
personal pasts;
of value

they are not burdened
by the weight of tragedy I know
is born in my voice.
Rewriting the history of pain,

for once I know
what I am trying to say.
Those who love shall love
no matter how the bodies join.

The sea turns in its bed,
carries shells in to shore.
However slowly the sun always
fills them with warmth.

•

How I wish all links could be true,
and truth the first wave
of trust repeated in the salt
light of each love.

How I wish I could
steel myself against the onslaught
of night. How often must I
watch the hail beat down

the garden of all I have
lived and desired.
Yet the soil breathes,
breathes without knowing.

Slowly it unfolds petals,
unfolds them forever.
It forever reveals
what is close to the centre.

Whether we live with them or without them,
identity and love are a harvest
of doubts whose seeds take root in
the right soil despite us

and grow.

1987: Four Poems from *West of Darkness: Emily Carr, a Self-Portrait*

GREY

Harris said: *Cast*
your Indian stuff aside,
find totems of your own.
And I did,
for he spoke
what I had left
unspoken in my heart.
When the forest was dry enough
I edged my way
down between the boles,
found solace
in the water-soft quiet.

And here I am again,
a latecomer this spring
to Heaven's gate,
the forest a tinderbox
locked against me.
A heavy mail of darkness
chains the cedars.
They cannot move.
Even their branches
won't ease back,
let me pass.
I could stand before them
a thousand years,
never know I'm here.

Sit on your camp-stool,
old fool, and think.
Get out your journal,

think a way in
between the trees.
These cedars are older
than Adam.
God had no voice and spoke only
in forms.
                                        'Forest,' 'tree,'
cones overlapping and wrapped
in darkness, impenetrable
as one's heart.
Now, drawn to the forest edge,
I am one of His thoughts—

It's almost dawn.
The first light rolls
off the cedars.
They shimmer, wet
windows, turn black-
green.
                        That little pine
in the foreground,
the first and last of this race,
could be the centre.
It shines from within:
bronze light cracks through
its crust of darkness,
a grey beacon.
                                    It draws me
into its cave.
I shall
burn there, untouched, unborn,
outside memory.

SAINT JOSEPH'S HOSPITAL, 1937

My heart, a knot undone with pain, forgot
a beat, the message cut. I lie awake,
my life in jars of paint. The thirst I slake
with tears is loss, a canvas stretched too taut
by years misspent, the will of God I thought
assuaged and framed. Totemic fir now break
through mist and gulp the dusk in draughts. I shake
with breath. A month of pain has cast my lot.

I lie awake. To live, the Doctor said,
the trees and sky must rest. My pain must rest.
A breeze afire with shades of summers past
now scents my room. Machine aloft my bed
I type them out, neglected coasts so blessed
with myth, the poles I sketched. They hold me fast.

FOREST, BRITISH COLUMBIA

More than one way in

into the forest. For instance
light carves
through a dense shell of cedar crowns,
its teeth gnawing

lower dark

branches into smooth dark scrolls,
into nimbus clouds
brightening over my head as I pass beneath,
any change in light

delicious

scent drawing me deeper
into opening
a path through undergrowth knit
closely to

the forest

heart, the swords of each fern
each whetted on
the stone cold of the need I always find
myself carrying. I look up: branches

sharp and interwoven

against a lightening sky—
I can never
separate what continues to exist....
Light falls over branches

curtain upon curtain

such lace the finest
needlework in all creation.
Its net harvests my dark,
smooths it into these wet

trees finding

a way into where I can see,
the forest like myself a fragment
of God, once unnamed,
now a leviathan suddenly gentle,

suddenly waking.

A SKIDEGATE POLE

Entering the sheer
exuberance
of sky

the forest rears
into crests,

unleashes

them through the cedar boughs,
whirling each crown.

Before the delicate ache
between waves
collapses them
one roaring into the other

quiet

falls,
subtly—a seed

of green
light
tumbling through darkness.
Listen to it

fall—

its genesis
endless

while the forest seamlessly
closes
over like water.

The shaft
light carves falling
wears the many
faces
the wind chisels.

Under the blade of each
gust
the shaft gives in
to the soft
wooden features
of dark.

Inside me
the memory of first quiet
wells,
its message

hieratic,
rising through fathomless
rings.

As waves of light
stretch
one moment of growth
into the next,

the skin of my many
faces
thickens to bark;

swaying
my quiet takes
root.

1990: Five Poems from *Great Men*

MY CELLOPHANE SUIT

I used to wear a suit of cellophane
snug and
clear as a surgical glove.

My mother grew it inside her
stomach and dressed me
in it.
When the time came

I popped out like a black
tap
dancer singin' *mammie*
at the top of
my lungs.

As a kid I shone like silver
under my mother's touch.
My suit buffed up
just right.
I was a bright kid, yes,

I was full of light.
When I was big enough
I outgrew my clothes.

I went to school.
But my suit of cellophane didn't
stretch and I felt

the strain.
Soon it had shrunk so much,
it pinched my groin.
Just once some jerk

one desk behind ran
his hand down the back

of my neck.
My suit of cellophane
went with a bang
like a balloon held
to a flame.

And with my skin
exposed like this

it's all guesswork .

GOODBYE TO ALL THAT

At certain freakish seasons,
when the wind shears leaves from branches
or when pools of rain throw back
to the eye remnants
of floating newsprint
and the underbellies of new shoots,
                                        it strikes me
to staple hand-scrawled posters
onto houses boarded up between Somerset W. and the Museum,
Laundry Land's bulletin board, and fences
that cloister worksites
and the playground at McNabb Park,
                                        fix
time, date, and purpose
of the sale, promise rain or swelter
to spread soon-to-be-cast-off treasures on makeshift tables
for the pleasure of nimble
fingers I do not know.

Amazing how clothes that no longer fit
or were ill-fitting when first tried
attract buyers;
                        marks of disuse and split seams
open to interpretation by those who don't understand why
I chose them, these shirts and ties
hats and scarves thrown aside by seasons I no longer know.
Imagine wearing the leaky Wellingtons I used for clamming,
tuxedo pants for graduation long gone in the ass.

Careful with the set of dishes my sisters handed down,
one to the next, when they got married.
Like theirs before mine,
                                lovers fed from them
and drank wine, broke plates

and cups in the throes of love that are best forgotten.
Whoever buys them, may those they love
at worst preserve their present state of incompletion.

It is difficult to set prices
for sacred objects I may not miss.
                                        What is recurrent
in this season that makes me want
to leave myself open
to valuation by others, the downward spiral
of negotiation over bargains
they will hide in turn on their own back shelves?

The sky is cloudless and bonfires spice the afternoon.
After the sale, the proceeds jingling
in my pocket, we will walk, you and I,
the Canal spread like slippery coins beneath the copper sun.
Should I spend it all
at the Black Cat?
                        I will raise my glass,
drink to the hope that little
in my past can ever do us harm.

GREAT MEN

Great men have slept
in each other's arms: Rimbaud
and Verlaine;
                    Auden and Isherwood;
and maybe Michelangelo
warmly carved David's thirst
for women in
the marble thrust of some half-forgotten
lover's unforgotten
thighs.

     Or Whitman leaning easily
against the wall in a rough
Philadelphia tavern, his vision unrealized
in a young man's slender hips
and the barmaid's breasts,
his lovers' quick movements singing
like two
birds in a cage.

                    And Cavafy dreaming of the ease
of the Greeks unreachable across the terrible blue
Mediterranean of the last
two thousand years of his privation.
And Crane jumped ship and Mishima lost his head.
And I think of crazy Tchaikovsky returning always
to his half-crazed wife.

                              And there are others
who lie in the quiet arms of their
lovers, their bodies intimate,
hidden behind drawn curtains in London,
Vienna, and Prague,
Sydney, Tokyo, and Montréal.
This is more furtive than clothes

a moment shed and the single
passing of hands over one-night flesh.
This is the hand
held out in dangerous recognition
again and again.

This is the hand that becomes
two hands undistinguished in the gentle
search of caressing
and caressed giving rise
to lips on nipples, on stomach,
and penis hardening
against anus.
This is courageous.

This makes men
ghetto themselves in the arms of women
they do not love.
                                        This makes men
who love their wives want
to tear out their hearts,
the clarity of desire unobtainable
as stars.
                This makes men walk,
walk, walk

the bitter mile along the sea,
the tide ponderous,
the sky ponderous,
the walk home ponderous,

the key in the door useless
as the rooms each one
leads to.
Desire turns to lust in the thin
fingers of their cowardice.

AU GARAGE, MONTRÉAL

On the dance floor gyrating limbs.

When two or more gather
fear slips like a shirt from heavy shoulders,
tangles about chair legs.

Exposed arms arc through smoking air.
On each: bleached hairs
glassy against winter tans—

feathers lying rhythmically
in one direction, the beat
linking eyes, the body wanting

proof. Faces unshaven, grim with sweat.

•

Around us lights wheeling like hawks.

Beside me at the bar a man fingers
his beer, digits of one
lit-up hand tonguing the amber

neck where it curves toward the rim,
that tight anus.
A presence descended among us

in jeans and damp T-shirt, cigarette
pack golden through a turned-up sleeve,
he talks, he waits, he listens:

competing strobe lights fragment
all who turn toward him,
our striated bodies anecdotal,

predestined.

•

Through the entry men come and go

worshipping Mishima, Marilyn Monroe.
Wayward merchants of wayward flesh,
like a cartel we gather,

disperse, reassemble, and assess,
here, where judgment strips to the skin,
a sleek figure dancing for pleasure

on a bar stool, tranced visage
lolling on a virile neck.
Here we license

hearts fresh to human trespass.
Eyes meet as do hands and lips,
tentative, our bodies escaped.

And each night's doorman is never death.
His winged smile, tender
whether he takes or holds up our coats, hints

blithely: *in situ* at last.

NAKED HEARTS

Avec un coeur nu dans ton coeur rempli,
I will live,
the body's audacity to be learned,

meeting the first evening,
fingers linking somewhere along Saint-Denis.

Shall we stop at Café Nelligan
and drink in the warmth
of candles and mulled wine?

Or shall we walk on

until our eyes meet,
until each insinuation of the flesh

spins us closer,
our gradual skins flowering
with slow desire?

Cross this threshold with me,
discover how deeply the city sleeps.

No one hears us reduce
ourselves to bodies changing
shape in the vivid dark.

The grief of our bodies
retells the world's body of grief.

Draw me between your thighs,
into the search
of mouths, the orifices of love.
Listen to the soft cadences of my sighs.

I had forgotten how my grief
rises, how quickly it wells up
under the tongue's roughness.

Release it, nest in my arms.
Lying here,
the Earth is caught in a split-second calm.

I no longer fear to be a man
and we are lovers whether our lovers
are women or men.

Avec un coeur rempli dans mon coeur nu,
lie beside me.

In this century those like us
refuse like us
to live as if we have never been.

1993: Two Poems from *Notes toward a Family Tree*

IN THE YEAR OF

This is not the woman you met
on the great jade steps
of the Imperial Palace Museum.
That woman you talked of
only once, then she was lost,
left among the loot of China;
a figure stopping a moment
on a staircase, a lacquered gate,
your smile and too few words.

Who is this? This woman
shy beside you at my door?
Yet another from the same
tumid summer in Taiwan?
One more of those who fell
so briefly down beside you,
so gently into the scented
sheets of several afternoons?

This one does not seem yet
a lover. She does not yet
take your hand and count
each finger as if distracted.
Arranged on the couch arm so
modestly beside you she stares
at the odd trees coming
into leaf against my window.
Half aloud she wonders
if such trees bear fruit.

She must be the one
I have long expected.
The one you obliquely mentioned.
The one who stepped from
behind a screen of air
at a bus stop and gave you
the right directions.

In a picture I once saw
of you, you are sitting
with one arm around her
on a terrace spread
above the snaking heat
of streets in old Taipei—
your glance toward the lens
a rising thread of incense.

Right now your untangling gaze
is wound up in the movements
of her hands. Resting two fingers
a moment below one breast,
she studies the clouds
fret across the deepened sky.
She notices the Ming designs
billowing through the curtains.
Quietly she begins explaining
the good luck of the peach,
the peasant meaning
of its slight heart shape.

METROPOLITAN LIFE

The straw hat I left in a New York restaurant
fit with a difference; without it my eyes
squint at the late summer twilight cutting
down through the ginkgoes lining Fifth—
the brim a screen through which I strained the world.

The high-strung woman with whom I split
a bottle of imported Italian bitters
would lean back in her wrought-iron chair
and, on occasion, laugh, hands folded safely in her lap,
the table between us a banquet spread
for those who live on little at the city centre.

That night, for the first time, we walked out
into the explosive dark, the air sentient
with leaves impatient to fall, to unroll romance
like a minefield beneath our feet. On such walks
the heart lifts anchor, veers from port toward the Red Sea.
At that moment Flight 007 took off for Seoul from JFK.

The night before, watching a rerun of *Dallas,*
we wondered yet again who the hell shot JR;
across Manhattan, we, the numb in one another's arms, marvelled
how fate connived to reanimate the machinations of his flesh.
Meanwhile refugees pour through the Khyber Pass;
Somalia burns its emaciated Ethiopian dead.

For seven weeks crowds at the Met milled through
rooms of Édouard Manet; a century earlier
he struggled with the idiosyncrasies of the everyday—
the slope of a woman's back while she took her bath,
a girl in mourning, children at the Tuileries.
In him alone did we recognize a world,
its brevity held in balance between good and evil.

On the radio this morning Tony Bennett left
his heart in San Francisco, but I would bring
mine back. There is enough loss.
An airliner is shot down over the Sea of Japan;
people are displaced from this Earth by war and starvation.
A man and woman walk past the United Nations
into the night, part, wonder where they are.
Who will recover the print of tiny flowers
she left in a midtown restaurant beneath his hat?

1994: Seven Poems from *Designs from the Interior*

CITY IN THE FOOTHILLS

What grows into my body
is night,
the ink prairie sky above the dull
sodium glow of the street lamps as I
walk home
along the road I used to take
to and from school, sun setting
early or rising late in this cool country;
the houses snaking down the hill
on either side as I walk
familiar as the cold door keys clutched,
pulled from my coat pocket.

On this road my body altered
without me noticing.
My shoulders sloped forward;
my stride lengthened from the walk
back and forth, back and forth,
tuna sandwiches my mother made
squashed by books
with broken spines in my backpack.
Back and forth, home
through this spreading suburb,
arms swinging, eyes wandering
under the wings of a chinook.

In the distance the hills
are fallen horses, dusky brown in late winter,
their coats purple-brushed
each spring by the first crocus.
They will never rise from the sleep
they fell into when I was six,
the first day of school.

Let them dream,
for they have worked hard
pulling the carts that stood the weight
of provisions uncrated
before the mountains as this city grew:
the mahogany table and chairs,
photo albums, and maps I unfolded
with my sisters, with my mother and father.

DELIVERY

He is approaching.
The horse lumbers before the milk wagon,
one shod hoof before the other,
the gravel in the alley
grinding like teeth
as he dawdles between
stopping, waiting, and starting.

The milkman always catches up.
In his metal carrier
the neighbours' empties gleam,
secrets they trade
for cheese, whole milk,
and cool oblongs of butter.
The bottles blur as the man
leaps into the hold,
dark as any cupboard
or hiding place I have known.
Suddenly he jumps down
into the heat of late morning.
The wagon rocks,
urging the horse forward,
joints cracking as he shambles,
stops a few houses closer.

A few houses away
I wait outside the back gate.
Slats of white
flash as it swings,
creaking behind me.
The breeze teases
the cowlick I wetted down
quickly after brushing my teeth.

Next to my heart I hold
a shiny quart bottle scrubbed
clean by my mother;
it is embossed with my handprints.

I stand in the crabgrass
restrained by the fence,
a knee-high jungle loud with bees.
Around my left ankle
my mother knotted a hankie
to take away yesterday's sting.
I loosen the knot
and peek.
The sting turns into
heat-dazed butterflies
weaving across the cloudless
blue sky of the cloth.

In my hands the bottle sweats.
My thirst emptied it;
for now it is brimming with sun.
I could catch ladybugs inside it,
stuff it with grass.
But I am waiting.
The horse is approaching;
the wagon's approaching.
I will trade this
emptiness with the man
for milk my mother says
I need to fill up my bones.

PHYSICAL

This hand—
what it uncovers, your breathing
as I examine you
downstairs in the airless basement, shirts pulled up
for the plastic stethoscope we should have
long ago outgrown, underwear and shorts
about our ankles, as we take turns
lying with knees
apart on my father's camp cot.

Already we seem older.
Hair wispy as your grandfather's
has begun to shiver where you want me
to probe you between the legs.
I run the cold
face of the stethoscope
below your belly button and listen—
your eyes follow my hand,
my lips tremble.

This is how we have come
to acknowledge the body, not through
words, which are dangerous,
but through touch and gesture, hours of playing
out the story of the patient
who does not get well,
a game we never tire of
as we search, play
with other boys, looking for cures.

It has begun to scare us how
the penis wakes
at random, freed from pants by zippers,
side by side, you and I
leaving in the snow one cold winter night
such signatures twined and steaming.

This hand—
it embraces mystery, the hungry
language of involuntary

nerve endings as I lie back on the cot,
not for the first
or last time, while above me
a yellow stethoscope that tells us
nothing
shimmers against your naked chest.

ECOLOGY

You were always and never the boy next door,
sat in the desk behind mine,
walked home with other friends, half a mile up,
the hills shaken out like ragged burlap
above Capri Avenue where you lived.
In high school, I loved you
with a passion I could not call love,

instead called ecology,
the 3 square feet of hillside we catalogued
under wind-torn sky, prairie
crocus and grasses, two types of sage,
red ants quick as blood, aphids nuzzling yellow
buffalo beans and pupa dreaming
among the roots, a world
to be sampled, an uncommon love.

We sat together, but apart
with other boys at lunch, played cards,
repeated the same jokes
about the girls in class.
I would look across the littered table
while you laughed; a faint
hint of beard flushed your cheek.

You found my letters after school
among your books, your gooseneck lamp
trained on paper unfolding
nomenclature you understood,
but never answered.
Instead you lent me your field notes,
sheet after sheet of precisely
drawn foothills plants.
I pored over them like pornography,
each life cycle labelled and explained.

You were always and never the boy next door.
Now we sleep with men in different cities,
collect them with an ardour not quite
expert, but studied nonetheless.
When a man lasts more than a few nights,
I might describe the secrets of that hillside
where nature touched us first,
describe how, over a lifetime, 3 square feet
of friendship become a country,
its soil wild and fruitful with desires
sampled, then elsewhere spent.

THE MAN FROM GRANDE PRAIRIE

Already you have lived under my skin
longer than the one late hour when I held you in my arms.

You drew the curtains and we were in a room
of touch; my sightless fingers looked
for the way inside you, my hands like lanterns
shining down a forest road on a moonless night.
They amazed you.
Your breathing told me that my touch was light.

That night before I met you
my hands were cold.
I had walked through this cool
Ontario city to where I met you,
by chance, in a bar without a coat.
When at last we danced,
we danced under a cloak of coloured lights.

Your body in my arms warmed me
with its residue of clear Alberta air
that lingers on my hands.
Your sweat reeked of poplar wood and campfires,
of rounds sung about the flames
with laughter and an untuned guitar.
It reeked of the Rockies
overshadowing where I grew up.
I licked it off your skin,
your cock in my fist and in my mouth.

After we came, you told me
how you hate the northern town
where your mother bore you
and that you can't escape,
despise its pulp-mill workers,
their hard hats and calloused ways.

You told me of the man in Calgary
who loved you then turned away.
For months you've lived out on R.R. 1
and told no one; in that remote
and lovely land you must be crazed.

My hands left heat on your skin
that you could not escape,
the surplus heat of remembered
cities, of garden homes
and unfolding suburban maps.
The next day, instead of meeting
as we arranged in a restaurant,
we met by chance on some corner
smouldering with rush-hour traffic.
Not the parting you had wanted;
we shook hands, then you turned away.
Now, as you are flying homeward,
I will never get to ask.

We all carry a darkness inside us
that has nothing to do with
forest roads, cities, and moonless nights.
It is not what we are born to,
but it shadows forth within us
as we age, desire casting
silences longer than we can bear.
We all run before them, but must learn
to stop, learn to carry this darkness
toward each other with unblaming hands of light.

PARALLEL LANES

We meet underwater, swimming in parallel lanes.
Both of us rising out of the breaststroke,
hands forcing the water apart.
We meet like this, length after length,
our trained bodies dreaming
a way to each end of the pool and turning,
coming up for air to breathe only,
the black hair matted across your chest
a flag that rises, that falls.

Later in the shower room,
after all the other swimmers have left,
we exchange something more furtive than glances,
something more gentle than words
as we talk, soap lathered onto our skins
and into our hair, washed
off with such pleasure, a common
language of bodies released from their stories,
which we will tell each other over coffee
after we dress, underwear that is the beginning
and end of seduction, the well-worn jeans,
the red shirt that a sister made you
tucked in half-unbuttoned while drying your hair,
the dark flag of your chest unsettling
as you bend to lace up your runners.

On the steps of the Champagne Bath, we are suddenly ourselves.
Brightly coloured jackets resist the cold
air come between us as March blows off the river.
Walking into the Market, snow catches

in our hair like sparks, sparks that melt and go out.
Already you are telling me about some man
I will later watch you talk to,
leaning into the phone booth, laughing,
mouthing into the receiver: *I will be home soon,*
as you have been for eleven years.
Crossing a restaurant crowded
with empty tables and chairs with bashed-up legs,
you smile inwardly, navigate
among all the abandoned coffee cups
and the slow-burning candles between us.

Stripped of the heavy clothing of this snowy night,
I want to be held as the water holds you,
swimming in another lane toward and away.
I want to hold this man of yours as you do,
want to know, in one lasting embrace, how to hold a man
forever in the sure arms of this, my only life.

FOR THE BOY WITH THE EYES OF THE VIRGIN

Let me be your ice,

the boy says in the Texas heat,
black mestizo eyes,
broad face, bare-chested, barely sixteen,

says this to me
near Losoya and Commerce,
where I have been approached before

by a black mother for bus fare, an exhausted
daughter cranky in her arms,

in the hotel district, overlooking the Riverwalk,
its paved water-level
pathways flooding with tourists, flowers, and noise,

an attempt at urban renewal
where lovers meet
beneath the pecan trees after store owners
roll down the protective metal grills.

This boy offers to cool me down,
on a day hotter than blood,

when, dehydrated and sun-stroked,
all I want after hours

of pilgrimage to the four
tumbledown stone missions giving this
lonely city some kind of heart

is something cold—

I will take almost anything,
having stopped at this
snow-cone stand where he seems to have
waited all afternoon for someone
dazed and weary, ribbing

the girl who works it, who tries
to block him from me;
the scooped-out globes of crushed ice
she gives me for so little
staining my tongue cherry-red.

This cone of mired Arctic
purity smoking
in my hand barely slakes
my thirst and the boy follows

as I move on, wants to
guide me wherever it is I want to go,
back to my hotel if need be.
Let me be your ice,
mister, you're so hot, you better lie down.

The scored veins of his arms
are clotted with stigmata,
this smooth-chested
boy with the eyes of the Virgin
of Guadeloupe whose gaze
sun-crazed I felt
follow me from nave to nave down the poorly
marked Mission Trail and last night

in the bars along San Pedro.

Dark-eyed men who flew with the USAF
the only time they left Texas.

Their looks make my blood
tingle with cayenne, these grounded
flyboys who like to two-step at the Silver Dollar,
who joyride in pickups after hours
all the way down to the Alamo.

And this is where I leave him,

at the monument to Col. Travis and Davy Crockett
and the 189 white patriots
who were not the only ones to fall.

Something marketable in San Antonio's history
not lost on him
as he starts to explain,

this aggressively beautiful boy
who, as the twilight
breezes lift stray
newsprint from the gutter,

looks hungry as well as cold,

who I refuse with money, not knowing what
icy current of death
he might also carry in his blood.

1998: Five Poems from *Sweet Ellipsis*

TOUCH-SCREEN

Welcome to my museum;
I am its artefact,

rescued by a curator with a good
eye from the backlog.
I bear an accession number,

not the old kind

tattooed on the wrist, but one stamped
into a cracked S.I.N.
card tucked in my wallet.

To anyone
unsure of what I am

here to represent,
my exhibit label points out how
characteristically tight

these faded jeans fit,
conforming

to my hips from an afternoon
of lying
stoned in the bathtub while some mother
whines at the door,

just another typical mendacious and lazy
long-haired child of the 70s.
The past

piles up everywhere—

quadraphonic sound, black light
posters, love beads,
earth shoes with negative
heels—indescribable by the usual

tags.
Besides, who reads?
The narrative is touch-screen,

these ribs.
And my penis: pure living

history hanging representatively out
of sight for as long
as I can remember, the first

interactive, now retrievable
and on display
at the whim of the visitor.

Today it is more than ever
responsive to touch.

I am a demonstration, every gesture nothing

less than semiotics, vicarious orgasm.
Watching the monitor mounted
on my neck

in place of my head, anyone

can scale the erotic
mountains
of my youth with pitons and rope, set

the speed of the stored

full-motion video—pure pornography—and climb
a rock face to the rear
of a comely
unselfconscious guide, his hard

breathing and curses whispered through snug
headphones, the audio
flirtatious, leading all the way

to the summit, the legs

of the Bow Valley spread wide

far below,
the Vermilion Lakes pink as skin
coursing in time-lapse through channels where moose
feed at twilight.

Technology allows the viewer
to zoom in or pull back.

And the sky,
whether it is real or not,

is the limit.

SARANAC LAKE VARIATION

> *I am mainly preoccupied with the world as I experience it,*
> *and at times when I would rather be dead the thought that*
> *I could never write another poem has so far stopped me.*
> *I think this is an ignoble attitude. I would rather die*
> *for love, but I haven't.*
>
> —Frank O'Hara, September 1959

Boxing Day 1993,
alone in my hotel room, reading
City Poet in the bath, (Bruce calls it
Brad Gooch's *I-do-this-I-do-that* life
and times of Frank O'Hara),
water hot and replenishable to my armpits,
toe blocking the overflow,
                                        and I think of you,
far away in New Brunswick (yes, it *is*
important), with your family, the frozen
Northumberland Strait outside
the window a ghost looking in
while you dine, no doubt,
on leftover turkey and mince,

and I think of Frank's love of the unrequited,
the longing

and invention he needed to articulate his poems,
those windows.

The Adirondacks rise outside my hotel window
into grey light, your chest pushing
against my hand last
week as it slid, a cross-country skier
                                        down and across

the plateau of your stomach, fingers coiling
round your cock in clouds of snow,
my mouth a blizzard about to
                                                touch down, which you
sometimes becalm, afraid (I am not sure)
of my teeth or tongue or what
you may or may not pass on,
the springs of your bed
sighing beneath us, a stand-in
in some *ménage à trois* (I said to
make you laugh), though you want this
variation (not the laughter)
hidden from all those who listen.

Something Frank never worried about
in the 50s, the emergencies he meditated in
the midst of (despite McCarthy)
more *automatisé,*
generations of Abstract Expressionists at the Cedar
apprehended by his conversation and surreal
appetite for straight men, Irish
tears and bourbon, jazz,
                                                spontaneous poems
dribbled unrevised
on the backs of coasters in 10 minutes flat
for someone in their circle (the nerve
of those private
asides drawing the rest of us—his future
readers—in) before he headed out
onto Eighth Street drunkenly at 2 a.m., alone or not alone,
love with a Manhattan skyline a sentimental
disease of his cruisy,
immunodeficient (i.e. vulnerable) spirit only.

In our time love has become a slogan, a cold
wind howling in the streets
of liberation, something we keep before the courts,

a paper coolly delivered at seminars
worldwide where doctors,
scientists, and activists compete
on how best to shield the sick
and unsick from variations mutating
like wind-sheer in the blood and in the minds
of those who wish us
dead, hate
no less virulent than in Frank's time—
only how the language is used
has mutated,
has kept mutating since his death,
though how it mutates and the aesthetics
of mutation (a.k.a. The Tradition)
allow it, chimera-like, to persist in secrets.

Frankly speaking, as Frank would say, the discourse
from the bathtub should be direct
(hot or cold), i.e. __________,
find me irresistible, though I can be
a klutz, for instance nearly
dropped Frank in at least once so far;
the sodden pages might well have frozen
shut and cut his story short
(which would be sad since he died
(not from love—on Fire Island
a beach taxi ran him down) at 40).

This afternoon the wind has been too
unspeakable and crystalline
for anyone to skate for long on Mirror Lake.
The wind-chilled glass in my window
changes steam rising from the bath
to frost and now I can't see
myself, so am lost and ready to confess
that I, Frank's pale imitation (Bruce says
I echo his looks), wasn't straight

about you with John and Lorraine
this morning over breakfast, invoked you
not in conversation by name
(who am I protecting?),
only as someone's son who came here once,
not my lover lured by the fleeting
weekend leaves with your parents to stay
in this hotel, perhaps sleeping comfortably
in the roomy bed where last night I dreamt of you,
where you might have once
dreamt about someone like me,

anticipating our bodies, a variation
on the unconscious,
therefore primordial and beloved.
Desire takes many forms, but perhaps what
is unspoken cannot be
edited out and (sweet ellipsis) becomes
the content of the poem—
                                        windows blown out
by winds loosening chance
ecstatic needles from stands of white
pine on some far shore even
a city boy like Frank would walk along
for lack of anything else
new to write about.

PUSHING UPSTREAM

Below my window, men in boats
are blasting a way into the river, moving

up from the mouth,
slowly, charge by charge,
                                        exploding the myth
winter suspends over the current,

ice thick and green enough to bear my weight.

I wanted to believe in its permanence,
an opaque
body stretched out on its stomach, a man fast asleep,

sealing in the sweet
stagnant rancour of fish spawn and river weed,
frogs dropped like cold stones
to the river bottom, flesh made ice.

But the men below my window are insistent,
blasting a way in,
making room for orange
motorboats, blasting caps and life jackets,

boys at play in the snow-melt, inducing the thaw.

Their bodies sweat, give
shape to loose clothing as they kneel,
tap in another charge
just far enough from the edge.

I wanted to believe in the ice,
no matter how thin and cold,

and now I must live with
the gap between
each explosion and its shattering report,

men silently running well back of the spray
of ice shards
and the approaching

open: the man

with the lithe body who once
fell asleep in my bed,

how he could never give enough
to me, except his own
guilt, not even the chance
intemperate spasm of his penis's flume.

And now I must live with
the aftershocks, the immediate

shuddering cracks in this love I have for him;

how they flash

through his absence with the presence
of another, of anyone
who explodes this layered

green myth: you, lucky
fellow
in a motorboat, pushing upstream.

CONFIDENTIAL

When I bent
to pick, my hands
came away red and wet

—Margaret Atwood

In blood we trust, its integrity
channelled, a power grid

of veins,
those neutral carriers.

What is tested and pronounced clean.
What we want not always kept within

the speed limit, the streamlined
body dripping with desire,

sodden with such honesty, rosy
and watered

as well-tended garden soil.
Leaning on the rakes, our bodies

both contained and containing
worlds governed by something

internal, not merely mutual
rules of the road,

but an impulse rising
above the genetic,

above that surgical bypass
of the city where we find

ourselves living no matter what
wildernesses lie

beyond the civic boundaries,
though one or two of us

still have the confidence to subsist
from the land, raise

our own strawberries, which bleed—so she
said: a blood instinct

for survival (and strawberries) on our own terms.
Such heartiness

fortunate and outside the ever waning
listening area of the CBC,

its signal weakened, information
a newsroom virus.

In blood we trust,
only now to distrust.

Prejudice leaking into the stream
of conscience

no longer containable by our veins,
the garden flooding with intent.

Do not name us
and our blood will testify

at your inquiry,
establish who has blood on whose hands

no matter how we were swept off
course, our cars

carried from the freeway
and much farther

downstream toward our final destination
than any of us had planned,

with no chance for factory recall
since nature has acted.

And do not blame us
because we have

lost the freedom to bleed,
those among us who cling to uprooted

trees and hydroelectric pylons,
the cut lines

snakes cinched about us, bleeding
venom and fire, our futures

dangerous, outside the reach
of the sharp grappling

hooks of your half-hearted
rescue boats, our consanguinity

in doubt—just like
the others who slipped free

of their seatbelts while no one
was looking, only to become

trapped bloodlessly underwater
in rapidly leaking

interiors of air, those vacuums.
Take us

into your confidence.
We are innocents, every one

of us (*in blood we trust*), and like you
betrayed, the credulous

love of the earth still larded
under our bruised

and ragged
nails.

THE CRISIS OF LYRICISM

His neighbour frozen before her white
garage door glinting
in the withdrawn Michigan sunlight, a foretaste of snow

Brodsky before us in the classroom
telling stories

the allegory of how he came

to understand Frost as America's foremost
poet of terror, newly
exiled from Russia and teaching in Ann Arbor, this scruffy

brutally sensitive man, ten years later, lounging before us
chain-smoking Marlboros, pausing between haphazard
drags, "Take Five" vented
down through the floorboards from some dimensionless

practice room above...
the national anthem of whatever

united states, it doesn't matter which—
according to Brodsky—
liberty

more or less

an improvisation ever since he first
heard Brubeck jamming
under the stars and sickle moon in Leningrad, the ember

of Joseph's cigarette leading
us toward the blank

face of his argument, a woman
frozen
before her garage

door for almost ten minutes without hoisting it open,
shedding
no light on the clutter within.

I found myself imagining
chainsaws, bicycles, the Toyota
idling in a trance

of exhaust, waiting to be let in,
the garage door blazing against the deluge

of vermilion and harvest, the empty
maples about her, a clutch
of children ready to be taken away by the school bus.

I pictured Brodsky opening his living-room
blinds to watch,
the voyeurism that is neighbourliness,

that is art.
For all I know

she cut the demeanour of a mannequin
modelling
slacks at JCPenney, fallen
leaves artfully displayed at her feet, Brodsky watching

her consider what can merely be guessed at,
something stories only can
find words for "bicycle," perhaps or, "chainsaw,"
the word "Toyota" waiting to be let in.

Or will anyone really believe that?
In today's version
the woman might well hoist the door open, twenty years later is

about to drive in
to humours too private to grasp.
Adjusting the rear-view mirror, who does she

see loitering at the end of her driveway?
If she had any brains
she'd throw the car into reverse without thinking and floor it.

Have I kept her idling against her will?
And what about Brodsky?

Goosefleshed by that cool and stateless
autumn mapped
inside Frost's America

who is able to speak?

2001: Seven Poems from *Hypothesis*

WATERSHED

Everywhere the blue and green world.

Your button-down shirt and corduroys.

The disparate shores of the park joined by opposed lanes
of traffic above the river below, the currents
of noise and moving

lights on the bridge easing as we enter the cloudy
starred bowl turned over the park's laconic
band shell, the banks

of the torrent we walk along
thrown wide, the open

neck of your shirt
disclosing a weedy insinuation

of chest hair, the copper-green veins of your throat, and aspen
coloured eyes looking downward, stirring the cold
backwaters of mine.

While a blue heron lifts greyly from the bird sanctuary
mallards with matte malachite
heads alight beside us in a moonstruck eddy
of rushes, assumed processional one or two swim away from

each season, away from the cycle
of the arbitrary, webbed
feet feyly waving *adieu* like we do (or

is it "hello"?)

Hello, stranger, hello—

Against the riverine sheets of my bed the frontiers
of your body exposed with
dexterity

terrain not undisturbed before we met but still something I want
to attend to and tend—the very pith of you
sunburned, hay-stubbled, cicada-lyred, unfenced-in

ground some would call waste

renewing itself, delirious, verdant
humours rising
to my fingers, your bracken

patterned olive and bice

boxers large and loose upon your hips, tongue
leafing into mouth, timothy
sage, kinnikinnick—

this bed a raft of green, fresh-cut
logs shot
forward by the snow
melt of my for-now exhausted blues through

a city where some of us
grow afraid of
adding
                    nothing to the flow

but you say
we take nothing away

so without issue despite the love we commit.

We are living the new equations
of this aqueous
arboreal enlightenment.

Somewhere in the open water
of Hudson Bay, blue
is the hue of the future, millennial, a blue

ravished planet set

adrift in the heavens and seen
from afar, our fellow
men swept up in its whirl, perspectives over

whelmed in the greenwood beneath the azure
foreknowing
of dawn, their consciousness up-close and engorged.

So the green body calms the blue mind
briefly—still one reminds
the other of
its place in the whole.

Decline and regeneration are everywhere.

Everywhere the blue and green world.

HYPOTHESIS

Because positive was negative
because his body
was too full of antibodies

he let in

the cells of a baboon protected
by nature from whatever

makes him sick, killing him slowly
but still too fast.
He won't

go quietly

he says, he won't let any
one forget, his
body

a memorial in the making
to the other

men already gone, to the positive
men of the future, to the ones
who don't yet know, his will bodacious

unlike his nearly exhausted
T-cells so far

still

able to fight the routine, opportunistic
illnesses of the soul
his positivity has invited in.

Though he wants to be negative
it's not in his nature
anymore to

be anything *less.*

Because positive was negative
the baboon was killed
its resistant
cells tentative inside him, resident

aliens.

Are these the foreign agents every
body fears?
Their rumoured
inhumanity might already

covertly circulate among us.
Some panic

the secrets of the flesh we are
beginning to unlock
too easily

let in the future
the cells

of an animal sampled
by those who kill
because they have no choice

because they require a specimen
for further study, data
to write up

once

they have risked everything to
turn something positive
negative
their careers

suspended in the blood of a man
who took chances
in bed he recognized

too late, the trust between lovers
a probability except
by intuition
even doctors at one time had no

reason to doubt.
The scientific method.

Those ethical, clean
cut guys
in lab coats, they look nervous.
They find it hard

to be objective, are trained to
be optimistic
but feel left out

by anyone with a positive
attitude who has
learned, with sacrifice, to keep all

affirmation to himself.

AT LINDOW

I found you
among the mosses beyond the airport where new
runway landing lights lead to
arrival

the excavated layers
of peat revealing you
slumped forward, head pitched slightly
to the right
against your shoulder
naked, torso

misshaped by cumulations
yards thick, legs
missing, but only one
foot, ginger beard matted, a band of fox
fur round what is left
of your forearm, skin leathery, but smooth, tobacco
hued, cured
by centuries

of tannins in the dripping
sphagnum, a wound reopening

in the neck where we touched
as you were brought to
light, blood
long ago emptied

not into this watery
cold, almost airless
acidic bog

not flowing like traffic that now seldom
drains completely from nearby
roadways at night beneath stars no one
local will much longer know the names of

but collected
instead in some now absent
sacred vessel, the garrotte stopping breath
bleeding to and from
your lungs still knotted
thrice, savage, taut

about your neck, the skull's
base and crown a record
of the three grave axe blows blessing you while
you knelt, mistletoe

an aftershock hinted at
in the gut down through
time of the libation
you drank, airborne
pollens you ingested with a burnt
oatcake reminding me it was

spring when we met, this black
pool then pristine
remote
limitless, my body the whole unrecoverable
disenfranchised generations
since, carried

forward reincarnate beyond
Lindow Moss's vigorous
diminishment, your chest caved in round nothing
where belief once
surfaced, what ribs

remaining, soft as prophesy in the margins
of the bog, silent
witness to its retreat while transatlantic
flights touch down, your body devoted
given over

unlike mine has ever been, sacrificed
lover, to the release of what is
now waning moss, cotton grass
and ling

THE LIVING ROOM

> *Their rubbish alone was left.*
> *He was a vacant lot,*
> *he had become an exemption.*
> The squares of his mind were empty.
>
> —P. K. Page, "In Memoriam"

At the drop-in clinic near the centre
of town, I namelessly drop off
cotton shirts wrinkled as grey skin
to be slung on hangers and rifled through
by men whose flesh thins under the shaking
force of their scapulae, the deft
articulation of fingers a memory
as they thumb through gaunt fabric—
the colours so bereft
their rubbish alone was left.

Even as I drive away, a man buttons
wash-worn cotton about his body
as it vanishes, ribs rising through
jaundiced skin like stains as he breathes
haltingly, or so I think, driving away
with my fears intact, overwrought
about whatever might or might not be
deadly in my own blood, haunted
by my one parting thought:
He was a vacant lot.

Against my will, I slip inside
his flesh. Its slim vitality sits
amply on my shoulders as I drive uptown
every remaining bit of pleasure to be
had from it an undiscovered country
lying within reach, vague satisfaction
of desires unable to die
with him, the body a cairn, fog
lifting as I pause at an intersection.
He had become an exemption.

His world opens up: his death is my death
his love my love, the men he kissed
and held are men like us who've passed
through the ordinary arms of several others
dates in loose cotton shirts who drove us
home after the movies, each entreaty
to love made on nights when warmth was wanted.
Guys who made us feel safe not cautious.
One foolhardy night he fleetingly felt free.
The squares of his mind were empty.

ESCHER

One thing becomes another.

Two boys grow up
grow apart, live in different cities
day and night cleaving in two, clouds of geese overhead

migrating in opposed directions
sun- or moonlight moulting from their wings
and mirrored across the dark, rain-slicked roofs of slate

as one of us rises
from bed while the other sleeps
goose-down from our pillows tangled in our hair

like herring in the nets
of trawlers setting or heaving anchor in oceans
where the rivers below our windows empty, uncoiling like endless

opalescent snakes swallowing
their tails somewhere beyond the circle limit
of the horizon, an infinite labyrinth of fields spread in shrinking

multiples past the eye's dawn- or dusk-lit rim while the backwash
of high tide thrums far upstream against warehouse
quays like blood lured through

veins to the heart, its own circle limit collapsing
inward as memory spirals down a vortex
of expanding

particulars, which with every tighter downward turn more
minutely blur, dizzying the flesh aging in the arms
of those who love us, blind

weary flesh later sitting by itself to read the identical
books of Escher prints we gave each other
loosening with knives

those pages now swollen shut, the hand-stitched bindings silty
from the flood that leaks through the shale and mortar
of our shallow basements.

Ebb and flow overtook us.

SUNRISE, GRAND CANYON

We stand on the edge, the fall
into depth, the ascent

of light revelatory, the canyon walls moving
up out of

shadow, lit
colours of the layers cutting

down through darkness, sunrise as it
passes a

precipitate of the river, its burnt tangerine
flare brief, jagged

bleeding above the far rim for a split
second I have imagined

you here with me, watching day's onslaught
standing in your bones—they seem

implied in the record almost
by chance—fossil remains held

in abundance in the walls, exposed
by freeze and thaw, beautiful like a theory stating

who we are is
carried forward by the x

chromosome down the matrilineal line
recessive and riverine, you like

me aberrant and bittersweet, and losing
your hair just when we have begun

to know the limits of beauty, you so
distant from me now but at ease

in a chair in your kitchen, pensive, mind
wandering away from yesterday's *Times*, the ink

rubbing off on your hands, dermatoglyphic
and telltale, but unread

on the chair arms after you
had pushed yourself to your feet such

a while ago, I'd say; for here I am
three hours behind you, riding the high

Colorado Plateau as the opposing
continental plates force it over

a mile upward without buckling, smooth
tensed, muscular fundament, your bones yet

to be wrapped around mine—
this will come later, when I return

to your place and time, I know it, you not
ready for past or future, our combined

bones so inconsequent yet
personal, the geo

logic cross
section of the canyon dropping

from where I stand, hundreds
millions of shades of terra cotta, of copper

manganese and rust, the many varieties of stone—
silt, sand and slate, even "green

river rock," a rough misidentified
fragment of it once unknowingly

dropped when I was a boy into my as-of-yet
unsettled sediments by a man who tried

to explain how slowly the Earth meta
morphosed from my meagre

Wolf Cub's collection of rocks, his sheer
casual physicality enough to negate

all received wisdom, my body voicing its immense
genetic imperatives, human

geology falling away
into a

depth I am still unprepared for
the canyon cutting down to

the great unconformity, a layer
so named by the lack

of any fossil evidence to hypothesize
about and date such

a remote time by, at last no possible
retrospective certainties, what a

relief, your face illegible
these words when I began not what I had

intended to say—something new about
the natural dynamic between

earth and history, beauty and art—
but you are my subject, unavoidable

and volatile, the canyon
floor a mile from where I objectively

stand taking photos I will later develop of
the ripe, trans

formative light on these surreal
buttes to show you on the surface

how beautiful and diverse
and unimportant our time together

or with anyone else
really is—

ALL THAT ENTERS MUST PASS THROUGH —LOVE, THE VIRTUAL BODY, AND THE DECLINE OF THE NATION-STATE

"the interior has achieved another coup d'état"

This body: its constitution
beyond amendment and spastically tense, the upper
and lower chambers of the heart loud with perpetually ringing

bells and filibusters remembered from the past: my 60s childhood,
premature bedtimes, random Montreal mailboxes blowing
up into the October Crisis, house arrest

after school and the War Measures Act, *just watch me*
watch reruns of soldiers on Ste-Catherine pre-empt cartoons
in fast-moving black and white; a few more armchair assassinations

from Pierre Laporte to Kanesatake and the body is pure
instant-on, panicked, the gastric tract
lubricated by spoonfuls

of mineral oil, though less and less sense
of self slips by the body's apparently undefended boundaries
some tight-assed customs officer opening my briefcase with a smirk.

Who knows what anyone's wrongs and rights are anymore, inside or out
but let go and the dollar sinks, all systems borderline
immunodeficient, factories shutting down

and moving south. The body
and its seized-up conveyor belts: economic
depression become somatic, the remotest cells starving

for love, its currency inflated each time we kiss. The text abbreviated
in the flesh. But who has time to read? We watch
the country lose sight of itself.

•

The land we come to is the land we are

: your cheek an unregenerate clear-cut forest
: scalp the treeline receding
: eyes unsmelted ore strip-mined from the almost exhausted shield
: thighs slivers of prairie embedded like shrapnel in exploding suburbs
: ribs caging a discount outlet open 24 hours along some edge-city strip
: hernia scar the pulled-up tracks of a forgotten railroad
: loins the nearby lakes emptying of fish
: your heart a hole endless traffic rips out of the ozone

before it's gone I want to touch the land as it is.

•

Love, you want to leave
and I don't want to

let go. Montréal newspapers
spell your name in the skimmed headlines

an acrostic rubbing off in my hands
as I turn

the pages, sentiment
I can't wash off or away: smeared

toxic inks absorbed by an epidermis letting
things in and not out

living in a federation
its borders we say are not

up for negotiation (no matter how restless
the natives).

Inside the body, the psyche balances
thyroid and liver, brain and heart, the involuntary

nervous system impartial
unless thrown off

by something not quite withstanding.
In this cold country: Montréal a veritable

city of romance. How I would miss its snow
filled streets and packed

cafés with you gone
its museums suddenly empty and cinemas

recycling untold matinees of your absence.
Or my absence, for I would come

here no longer, unable to revisit
what we have now become, ghosts fitfully

asleep under the icy sheets of economic slowdown.
Once I would have given you

freedom of the city, would have
left my Métro pass and keys locked inside

an apartment leased in both our names before
catching a westbound Voyageur bus

left you to this life, to the divisive
polis at its heart you want to map, but I can't

leave you no matter where we draw
borders we won't discuss.

You are inside of me even when
I am on the outside, my ancestors since

the Plains of Abraham dug deep as compost into
the churchyards of the Eastern Townships.

My kind are taught to contain
ourselves, the imperial flourish

of an irritable bowel almost
Victorian in its habits.

•

All that enters must pass through.
Goods cross into Detroit from Windsor.
All that enters must pass through.
Eros uploaded with the food we eat.
All that enters must pass through.
Praise Gaia for the information highway.
All that enters must pass through.

•

In a 500-channel universe we are still
what we eat: stockpiled mother's
milk, CNN, takeout

pizza, 24-hour
shopping—the body

a network of networks: bloodlines
nerves and the intestines.
Hopelessly

interwoven for what centuries
must feel like, we let ourselves

let go of our limits, forget whatever borders
we did not choose and pick up
speed, our baud

rates pushing against those
of light and infinity until the connection somehow

fails and now, though you are gone, you are everywhere
projected against the blank screen
of my stand-alone

conscience or suspended
in memory. In the virtual, the sewage

of your desire washes through my less-and-less
carbon-based circuitry, your sweet
white noise I call up

repeatedly, all language
a simulation, sentient and magic.

Language heals, not love or medicine. Language is zero
and indivisible. Language lets go
of what it withholds

and gives up nothing
metaphor its viscera and lower colon.

Language is a microchip I collect (picking up
after the virtual cows) and burn
for warmth.

Our bodies speak
in languages we do not comprehend

yet we know who we are, distinct despite
the ether's apparent lack
of borders.

Let us go then, love
let us let go: something always dis or re

connects us to something.
What we singly burn
inside our bodies

joins in loose constellations
frayed networks of light ablur in the wheeling

night skies—the vaporous trails of our opposed
headlights archived for virtual broadcast
long after we race by each

other above
the river, its rank pixelated

flow between the bridge pylons star-crossed if oceanbound—
undercurrents pushing apart eroded
green shores

from whose viewpoints for a nanosecond
we look across to one another, then speed away.

AIDE-MÉMOIRE

First there was the dancer
                              then the refugee
                                                      then the gambler
and, counting back
wards at random, the anaesthetist
the adjuster, the interior designer known for
his way with gilt and feathers, the former military
adviser who still liked to trail men undercover followed
by the TV actor whose agent died afraid he would contract AIDS
the librarian who collated records about his lovers into alphanumeric
order (access points being size and chat name only), including Scam, the squeegee
boy with goose-fleshed skin who reeked of WINDEX, and Time-Lapse, the photographer whose life

blurred beyond the focused alchemic subtleties of black and white
unlike the lobbyist who remained uniformly shameless
or the statistician who was so neutral about
those he loved, he seemed no
more than average

so I left him for the substitute

teacher who set such a teaser of a quiz
I could not resist him, the choices so multiple
the possibilities for love were endless, or so I thought, exhausting

his pre-scored answers far too quickly
unwrapping the Eskimo
sandwich

the DICKIE DEE
ice cream kid sold me after
he quit my bed and dressed, he too was looking
for a father figure, someone to sleep with who makes him

feel safe

another literary man like me but perhaps one
more famous, who might read *The Odyssey* aloud to him in bed
before lights out, only to let us undock from our aimless, common moorings

I am the homeless man, *hypocrite lecteur*
you long to take in

who owns no baggage to pack yours into
who always needs a shower, my shoulders especially broad and dirty
with a back it takes hours to wash, who will slip on your sweaty CALVIN KLEINS

afterwards, if you want, and then let you peel them off, who will stay
for another night or another lifetime even if you don't
ask nicely, men are so

fidèle
je me souviens, I am

the one you recognize
from the bar who looks nervously away, the one
you confront when shaving, the peculiarities of your face hard
to summarize in the clipped, forever-young vocabulary of the companion ads, you are

the Winged Victory
                a Herb Ritts photo
                                Antonio Banderas
Tom of Finland
                you are negative capability
                                the lineman for the county

the towel boy at the baths
you are Alexander the Great
Dr. Jekyll
Dennis Cooper
the stocker at LOBLAWS
the objective correlative
you are PRESIDENT'S CHOICE

you are

the man in chinos at the street corner with a broken umbrella
your wet BROOKS BROTHERS shirt unbuttoned
at the neck, whom I

hesitate to give

directions, whose reflection
is trampled by the rainy afternoon
crowds of a city where no one ever truly lives.

WARHOL

with apologies to Wayne Koestenbaum

Hey there, Drella, it's me, Juan Baton: I erase you; I make you live—
the rod I rule with, diseased but social; its potency, prior to factory recall

an inflatable function of my body stilled, a balloon subtitling the freeze
framed, yawning torture of your films, my screen test becoming butcher

with time more shaved and tasty, a beefy snuff movie I am starring in
drugged-up, dazed, and odalisque, my cock a colostomy bag worn full

frontal and voiding desire, my insides all over your outsides, a loudspeaker
between my legs narrating blow jobs, no longer a microphone sucking

up passé modernist inhibition as it might have once, genteel and hidden
love then allegorical, asexual, allusive, now A-list, aphrodisiac, aphoristic

though, unlike you, I remain unAmerican, a foreign body, my ambivalent
alien destinies manifestly suspect and pissed away, but, hey, did I tell you

I aspire to baldness—so omega, so B-film, to be unwigged-out as you are
not, balling without tears, this kleptomaniac run-on sentence a time capsule

boyfriend after boyfriend after boyfriend after boyfriend after boyfriend
after boyfriend after boyfriend after boyfriend after boyfriend after boy

friend I lay end to end, the unmourned outlines of their flesh a compulsive
silk-screened orgy so empty and repetitious only the brillo-box scruples

of a museum could contain them—else no one will—longing contemporary
and unnarcissistic only in retrospect, the commercial properties of legs

and chests made abstract, dreamy citizens gone art-historical, devoid of life
RFK assassinated the day after Valerie shot you, his fifteen minutes almost

cancelling out you both, her anger no more notorious than your shopaholic
instinct to create, cannibalizing anything in sight, your scarred body a work

of the imagination I truss up until the lonely end, this breathy parasitic line
a film spliced with commas absent from your posthumous diaries, my own

angry voice made to slow down syllable by syllable, frame by jerky frame
as I project myself across the ready-made screen of your fame, ejaculatory

in homo slow-mo, a low-fidelity money shot so orchidaceous you organza—
a deadly improvisation you exteriorize stroke-free over my cropped-out face.

PATHETIC FALLACY

Annuals hardly ever endure our season, your hothouse seedlings
flirtatious and sickly as orphaned puppies, pot-bound when bedded

in shallow-raked, frost-straitened loam, its substrates an untutored
coalescence of sand and clay, the exposures seldom wholly felt

through—unimaginable light, watery uncertainties—all succulents
too tender for my very shivery Laurentian environs, moon-shaped

leaves straggling southwards, the stems anxiously moored
elongated and pale, the roots grasping at the errant nutrients

for a week's wild efflorescence, a racket of colour and scent
to arrest my attention, your gardening shears poised and a bud

vase washed when every gaping flower, just as suddenly, drops
seed—*how we persist in forced metaphor*—sun-drunk sepal losing

wet petals to the wind while our backs are turned, the thin limp
wristed stalks dying down into the rot-rich earth under snows

blown in from Alberta, evolution's appetite for deviation coiled
slackly inside those amnesiac seeds you aim into next year's bed

pathetic fallacy a trope for our phallocentrism, your scattered
penchant for feyly manicured blooms in contrast to my hardy

weediness, desire's other phylum, so perennial and wayward
in its rank cupidity, a network of thickening stems subversively

spread and prone to survive winters underground, unrepentant
and visceral, tenacious and wily, though you have tried hard

to eradicate its hold on my ground, challenging the rapaciousness
indigenous to this landscape, how it thrives in overworked soil

your poisons and admonishments, the civics of a carebound society
no match for the male body, the varieties of love it husbands

with rampant stoicism, anthurium and goldenrod, flamboyant
and irritating rivals unnaturally adversarial, the aggression

of their beauty soul-destroying to those who stand forbidden
to harvest them, who, unrequited, must bear their flourish

and wane, annual or perennial, domestic or weed, the bees
of the open field the final impartial terrorists, our bodies

at last sensing of their own accord exactly when the time is
ripe for stressed earth to lie fallow, *leaving the language to be.*

IN THE HOUSE OF THE PRESENT

I rise through the house, your dog at my heels
curious ears pitching forwards as we climb
landing window angled open, stairwell hazy
with the intense light of his barking as I enter
time's leaky vacuum, having not come to visit
in years, the hall dividing rooms not everyone
finds his way into, the way through coming
back to me, our parents still downstairs long
after we are meant to have fallen more deeply
asleep, dwindled voices ghosting me as I climb
our fathers staring into their ryes and water
while our mothers, so contrary, settle on how
best to set the table in the English manner few
pay heed to, silver against damask, carving set
poised on crystal knife rests—how they come
to sit next to each other on the Jasper Avenue
bus, what in the 50s makes them start talking
neither of us tries to guess at, our sisters at play
in the aisle, transfers made to points far beyond
the unexpectedness of our bodies, two sons
born two years apart, your mother bathing you
in the sink, skin pink against shining porcelain
until as you crawl up behind me I step back

our eyes downcast and lifting, meeting as I glance
over my shoulder, small foot squashing smaller
fingers into the Kashmiri carpet's deep crush
as, pulling at threads, the sun bleeds through
the clouds—what clouds—there always seem
to be clouds as I look skywards, unfurled bolts
of cirrus shading my eyes as slowly they open
to what we wake to hours before anyone else
your father in the eternal early light making us
breakfast, bread trimmed of crusts set to brown
in residues of bacon grease, he says, to fatten
us up—to what other purpose does anyone cut
into such yolks, two runny cow's eyes running
across the countryside breakfast china I find
misidentified pieces of in second-hand shops
your mother's voice turning down the hallway
with me until I open the door, blocks scattering
across the plain of the floor, the blown-apart
cities of the imagination no one ever moves
into, cities built on the unlit side of the moon
before you disappear ahead of me out the open
window with your camera, the case discarded
on the grass—there are still more images, still
more destroyed cities in your head to set loose
your mother, as she dies, anxious for me to set
them free with you, but older, imperceptibly

we live in atmospheres too heady for you or I
to detect while in the closet hangs the silver
space suit she one day makes you, the lucent
helmet you wear when I come around clouding
with your breath, though for now this sham orb
glows, clear and hollow on its briefly exposed
shelf, your dog clawing at the loose-woven rug
ragged by your bed, coiling into a sleep none
wakes him from until I am found in the kitchen
where our sisters dry the last of the remaining
day's dishes, clean faces caught in the plates
before they are packed into crates, vestigial
steam distorting the windows, and me wanting
to wipe it away, wanting the two of us framed
by the sill, framed and held by the willow
where you sometimes read with your father
among branches spreading low into twilight
under the sweep of sun-gilt leaves we play
unaware his book is closing, the most frayed
of catkins sifting down onto our heads, neither
of us ready yet to know what this house might
make room for and what it cannot, both of us
giving so little thought to our growing capacity
for inattentiveness or to our called-out names

DAYS OF 2004, DAYS OF CAVAFY

We Greeks have lost our capital . . . Pray, my dear Forster
oh pray that you never lose your capital.

—attributed to C. P. Cavafy by E. M. Forster

Away from the Houses of Parliament, wandering the streets of this ruined Confederation
neighbourhood under maples loosening darkness along a river where men could linger

past midnight in the chill, late-season air, I am anxious, thoughts wandering through
your far extinct quarter, not the squalid Alexandria you live in, but in the capital

you raise pediment by pediment at the rim of a great delta, city of golden arteries
buoyed by the mythic reflux of the river where millennia of young men heroic first

in their beauty, in their loyalty to the body, awoke in each other's arms, exquisite fallen
citizens true to the memory you keep fleshed out long after their city had abandoned

Anthony, long after your escape back from exile in Constantinople three years beyond
the less than transient music of British bombardment, an alien philihellene loafing about

town randy if circumspect, a youngest mother's son slipping out once she could drowse
only to muse past her death about the unreturned-to beds where after a game of cards

you would lie with changeable lovers in the Attarine district, shirts and trousers too briefly
shed, tattered, and for an hour revealing the wine-drunk gods your obscure city might

otherwise have kept out of reach, unimaginable men, their genders you would redress
years later make brashly presentable in a Greek so architectural, so arch in its pronouns.

•

Forster said: you begin from within, a life doomed by its devotion to transient things
youth, physical beauty, and passion—passion above all other: disreputable, excessive

in the "Greek" way of life as you see it, your true self admiring men in the street unseen
men whom you hope might still become and remain articulate in the artful, athletic tongue

of your ancestors, those inattentively schooled sophists whose bodies as discus throwers
adorn the coinage struck by adoring kings in commemoration of victories from Libya

to Antioch, wars thrusting far across Persia into India, the whole of an ancient world
inside you and you inside it, unearthed, the past intense with lust, the present imperfect

with men like yourself or worse, fallen or raised poor, badly dressed, whose inglorious
flesh so worn out by labour can still delight you, even in retrospect, however furtively

I look up to your second-floor balcony at 10, rue Lepsuis, where with a candle you sit
into the dark hours revising, observing the infrequent clientele of the first-floor brothel

arrive and go, your eyes delighting in the girls, virtuosos of technique and the earning
pleasures, a man in your forties guessing their names for no reason, your interest in them

idle: except by implication they never walk as others do through your poems, for down
through the history of Greece you remake from chosen bits of marble you have stayed

enamoured with the endless debauch of young men who linger, depart from your city
their desires voiced more often in the unseeming details you praise than in anything else

which I observe, though like you I am beautiful no longer, the best of your days like mine
spent rising heartlessly up through the arid Third Circle of the Department of Irrigation—

who ever sees you, Cavafy, who follows, walking your deflowered city, this Alexandria
where you have made all time simultaneous, yet seem always to despair of its passage?

•

Amazing how any of us can persist at being in more than one place at more than one time
sipping coffee in a bazaar while walking along a northern river gilded with brittle leaves

watching passersby, reliving the love we make with one man while at rest in the arms
of another, looking up from a newspaper on a city bus to retrace your steps, you a poet

born two centuries back, your path hidden, however memorably you may have one night
written about a man who years after your death might appear out of nowhere and act freely

from the study door I see you at work at your desk, yet I cannot see myself, a later man
unknown to the city I live in, a city not any less imperfect than yours, a city like so many

with a disposition for violence, its young men after unaccountable days still found in bed
with their heads bashed in, beautiful, naked, though there are times when men here seem

in appearance more able to act, citizens solemn, happy to observe men marry other men
though by such public vows they become invisible, respectably move out to the suburbs

however ambitious their anonymity may be proclaimed in the high court as it overlooks
the river and its currents, overlooks what might sink, what might get carried forwards

new housing starts pushing the civic boundaries past limits not even you or I could have
guessed, the men of every city made good citizens whom, sitting at your desk, you can

only envision as enviable devotees of pleasure—and they are, their self-induced beauty
however VIAGRA-enhanced, used up as it can be in your time, though some of us hope

desire may be caught, its decline arrested long before it is gone, each man a taxpayer
a contemporary Adonis constitutionally to be resurrected once a night in his own bed.

•

There are times, as you know, when a city remains a room, fortifications thin as the walls
street noises brought in on the coats to be shed, the weedy taste of the sewers on our skin

perpetual transients of the sheets, men from all over town inviting themselves in for an hour
for the night, not here on approval, beautifully unmarriageable but candidates for coupling

and culpable of nothing but the sweet relief of disappointment, like-minded citizens unable
to dissemble inside the room's time frame for long, skilled at keeping artful conversations

going only so far, articulately awkward, and knowing in their silences, the space of the room
immediately transformed into the space in their arms, each instant instantly archival, the eyes

recording unquestioned appointments—shelves lined with books leafed through or unopened
curtains drawn, chest of drawers randomly pulled out, narcissus dead in a glass on the night

stand, double bed islanded under a soft-lit fixture, shirts unpressed yet hung, as they are
meant to be, in a wardrobe—the air stale with memories no one is ever intended to know

though afterwards putting on clothes in the quick opposite order they were taken off
standing at the door in our socks, closing it behind them, we find ourselves wondering

wandering the streets behind them to the outskirts, musing on what barred store windows
they might browse, on where they likely stop for a beer on the way home, men we might

greet or ignore on the street for weeks afterwards, men who travel lives not too indifferent
to our own, travelling from Sparta to Thermopylae, from Sussex Drive to Albion Road.

•

Constantine, admit us: we all want to be Alexandrians, all want to be former exiles who stand
elegiac on our balconies and observe the street, knowing the ruined glories we anticipate

in transit below are behind us not ahead, knowing vestigial greatness may now lie elsewhere
knowing the cities where we live—any city—like Alexandria at last are enough, our attempts

at mediocrity sufficient to construct an urbanity, a backdrop for a life, golden boys in our arms
as irredeemable as those aging anywhere, as talented in excess, their inelegant candour found

foremost in the nerves, in the rapacity of their tongues, any unused callowness reworked later
by the heart, residual bits of history excavated over time, a communal transcript none of us

ever knows entirely—anecdotes retold in every city, in every suburb, in fragments not unlike
lifetimes you revise boldly, discretely, poems of a fallen city, of unchaste, eternal Alexandria

men of the future looking backwards as I look to you for a city map unfolding to relocate
where you are and where I might yet go, a man who walks along a river below the seat

of power in an unhellenic, plain-spoken country where few can still imagine there are gods
where I can pause along a lonesome street to give a stranger less unsatisfying directions.

ACKNOWLEDGEMENTS

I would like to thank the original publishers of the nine books and four chapbooks from which these poems have been drawn: Sono Nis Press, Ekstasis Editions, Penumbra Press, Quarry Press, House of Anansi Press, above/ground press, ECW Press, Viola Leaflets, Frog Hollow Press, and Brick Books, as well as Beach Holme Publishing and BuschekBooks, both of which published later editions of *West of Darkness: Emily Carr, a Self-Portrait.*

Thanks is also due to the many editors past and present of the magazines and anthologies where many of these poems appeared: *Backspace* (U.S.), *Canadian Forum, Canadian Literature, The Capilano Review, A Crystal Through Which Light Passes* (BuschekBooks, 2012), *Descant, The Drunken Boat* (U.S.), *Christopher Street* (U.S.), *enRoute, Evergreen Chronicles* (U.S.), *The Fiddlehead, GO Info, The Greenfield Review* (U.S.), *The Inner Ear* (Quadrant, 1981), *Literary Storefront Newsletter, Long Journey: Contemporary Northwest Poets* (Oregon State, 2006), *Lubricité, The Malahat Review, More Garden Varieties 2* (Mercury, 1990), *Open Country: Canadian Literature in English* (Nelson, 2007), *Outposts* (U.K.), *Prairie Fire, Quarry, Queen's Quarterly, Seminal: Canada's Gay Male Poets* (Arsenal Pulp, 2007), *Tickle Ace, Vallum, Westerly* (Australia), *Written in the Skin: A Poetic Response to AIDS* (Insomniac, 1998), and *Zymergy.*

The epigraphs throughout the book are from "Child's Park" by Ted Hughes from *The Birthday Letters* (Faber, 1998); *Nocturnes from the King of Naples* by Edmund White (St. Martin's, 1978); "Dream I: The Bush Garden" by Margaret Atwood from *The Journals of Susanna Moodie* (Oxford, 1970); ["Statement on Poetics"] by Frank O'Hara in *The New American Poetry,* Donald Allen, ed. (Grove, 1960); "In Memoriam," by P. K. Page from *Hologram* (Brick, 1994; the final line is quoted by Page from W. H. Auden's "In Memory of W. B. Yeats"); and "The Complete Poems of C. P. Cavafy" in *Two Cheers for Democracy* by E. M. Forster (Edward Arnold, 1951). The epigraph to "All That Enters Must Pass Through" is from a poem of the same name in my book, *A Poor Photographer* (Sono Nis, 1981). The italicized titles of poems from *West of Darkness* are also titles of paintings by Emily Carr.

Countless people have sustained me through the 35-year arc that this collection represents. I would especially like to invoke the memory of my mentors, Eli Mandel, Robin Skelton, and Anne Szumigalski as well as to thank Nancy Barton, Pam Barton, Richard Barton, Alison Beaumont, John Buschek, Barry Dempster, Rita Donovan, John Flood, Clarise Foster, Arlette Francière, Gary Geddes, Alisa Gordaneer, Robert Gore, R. W. Gray, Neile Graham, Mark Gallop, Lala Heine-Koehn, Bob Hilderley, Harold Hoefle, Michael Holmes, Anita Lahey, Ross Leckie, Christopher Levenson, Kitty Lewis, Miles Lowry, Norma Lundberg, Elizabeth-Anne Malischewski, Blaine Marchand, rob mclennan, Robert G. May, Kim Morrissey, Erín Moure, Shane Neilson, Sandra Nicholls, Nadine McInnis, Richard Olafson, Caryl Peters, Philip Robert, Bill Ralston, Doug Schmidt, Sue Schroder, Martha Sharpe, Andris Taskins, Lynne Van Luven, R. M. Vaughan (for his introduction, after many years of valued collegiality), Silas White, Eva Wynand, Derk Wynand, Ann York, and David Young. I am most indebted to James Gurley for years of advice and friendship, and for assisting me in the daunting task of making this selection.

PHOTO: HOLLY PATTISON

ABOUT THE AUTHOR

John Barton was born in Edmonton, raised in Calgary, and educated at the Universities of Alberta, Victoria, and Western Ontario, as well as at Columbia University in New York. Author of nine previous collections of poetry and six chapbooks, he has won three Archibald Lampman Awards, a Patricia Hackett Prize for Poetry, an Ottawa Book Award, a CBC Literary Award, and a National Magazine Award. Since 1980, his poems have appeared in magazines, newspapers, and anthologies across Canada and in Australia, India, the United Kingdom, and the United States. Formerly the writer-in-residence at the Saskatoon Public Library and at the University of New Brunswick, he has also taught at the Sage Hill Writing Experience and at the Banff Centre. From 1985 to 2003, he worked as a librarian, production manager, publications coordinator, and editor for five national museums in Ottawa, where he was editor-in-chief of *Vernissage: The Magazine of the National Gallery of Canada* and co-edited *Arc Poetry Magazine*. He has lived in Victoria since 2004, where he edits *The Malahat Review*.